One Hundred Things I'll Miss About Grateful Dead Land

# One Hundred Things I'll Miss About Grateful Dead Land

## CHRISTINE M. DUNNE

### DONEGAL PUBLISHING COMPANY

LOS ANGELES

Copyright (c) 2007 Christine M. Dunne
Original art by Richard W. Dunne
Illustrations by Brandi Brooks
Back cover photo by Jack Savage, Carmel, California, 1995

All rights reserved. No part of this publication, except for brief excerpts for purposes of review, may be reproduced, stored in a retrieval system, or transmitted in any form or by any means, electronic, mechanical, photocopying, recording or otherwise, without the prior written permission of the publisher.

# DONEGAL PUBLISHING COMPANY, LLC

1850 Industrial Street, #307
Los Angeles, California 90021
Email: editor@donegalpublishing.com
www.donegalpublishing.com
www.jerryland.net
Telephone: 310.598.6340
Donegal books are available from your favorite bookstore and amazon.com.

Library of Congress Catalog Number:
Publisher's Catalog-in-Publication Data
One Hundred Things I'll Miss About Grateful Deadland/Christine M. Dunne
ISBN 978-0-9788128-1-2
ISBN 0-9788128-1-6
Category description
1. Title
This book was written, printed and bound in the United States of America.

\*

Introduction

\*

    I was introduced to the music of the Grateful Dead when I was five years old; the result of having shared a room with my older sister. Later, I attended as many shows I could.

    Any fan knows the impact of not having any more Dead shows. I wrote this book in order to have a pool of memories to dip into whenever I want or need them, right at my fingertips.

    Sharing some of my memories about the many shows I've attended has helped me to deal with the loss of Jerry Garcia and the entire Grateful Dead experience. I hope it will help you, too.

    If you are unfamiliar with the Grateful Dead experience, perhaps this book will give you a glimpse into it.

    Here's to, "The Heart Of Gold Band".

-Christine Dunne-

# 1. Jerry Garcia

## 2. The length of the concerts.

3. The frequency of the shows.

4. The magnitude of inspiration from live Dead.

# 5. Falafels in the parking lot.

6. Getting that "miracle" ticket.

# 7. Homemade organic beer.

8. Meeting the largest proportion of the world's friendliest people.

9. Grateful Dead stickers.

10. Seeing the most interesting automobiles.

# 11. Hearing the jingle of bell anklets.

## 12. The fantastic fragrance in the air.

13. The colorful clothing worn.

14. Hackey-sack circles.

15. Spray bottles on a hot day.

# 16. Drum circles.

17. Ground scoring.

# 18. Reading witty bumper stickers.

19. Quality homemade jewelery.

## 20. The chocolate chip cookie lady.

21. Shopping for t-shirts.

## 22. Camping in-between shows.

# 23. Traveling to colorful places on tour.

24. The pre-show excitement.

25. Guessing the next song.

## 26. Grateful Dead newsletters.

27. Hearing about the sudden skyrocketing of local business when The Dead are in town.

28. Seeing the next generation of Deadheads attending shows.

29. Meeting the friendly animals at shows.

## 30. The visual effects at shows.

31. Waiting to hear "St. Stephen."

32. Running into people I know at shows.

## 33. Seeing tie-dyed baby clothes.

## 34. Being with so many Deadheads in one place, at one time.

35. Bouncing balloons around inside the show with fellow fans.

# 36. Seeing those cartoon flip-books sold at shows.

37. Seeing someone new being introduced to the Grateful Dead experience.

# 38. Hearing a song for every occasion.

39. The way the band would warn you about any bad "party favors" that might have been going around.

40. Hitch-hiking with a good friend or two up to a show.

41. Being able to score anything I want in a matter of minutes; i.e., an ear-piercer, pot brownies and a veggie burger.

## 42. Hearing and trading live Dead recordings.

43. Taking pictures of the band.

## 44. Successfully evading the "under-covers."

45. Hearing the first song of a set.

46. Seeing the spinners dance.

47. Taking my children to their first show.

# 48. Anticipating the band's next album.

49. Feeling about as comfortable as one can be at an event.

# 50. The fresh fruit cup lady.

51. The happiness in the air and all around.

52. Stir-frys in the parking lot.

## 53. Mail-order tickets.

## 54. Drum space.

55. Feeling like dancing to every song.

56. Seeing the Dead make the news.

57. The nurturing my spirit gets at shows.

58. Hearing "Cassidy" live.

# 59. Hearing "Terrapin Station" live.

60. The way the band would set up speakers outside for fans who didn't make it in.

61. The way the band provided a space for fans to record the band's music live.

## 62. Hearing Phil sing "Box Of Rain".

63. Hearing Brent sing.

64. The fascinating conversations one could have among the very interesting population of Deadheads.

65. Personal space being respected as the rule and not the exception, even while dancing.

66. Learning where the next shows would occur.

67. Hearing about how many shows other "Heads" had attended.

68. Hearing members of The Grateful Dead giving some of their rare interviews.

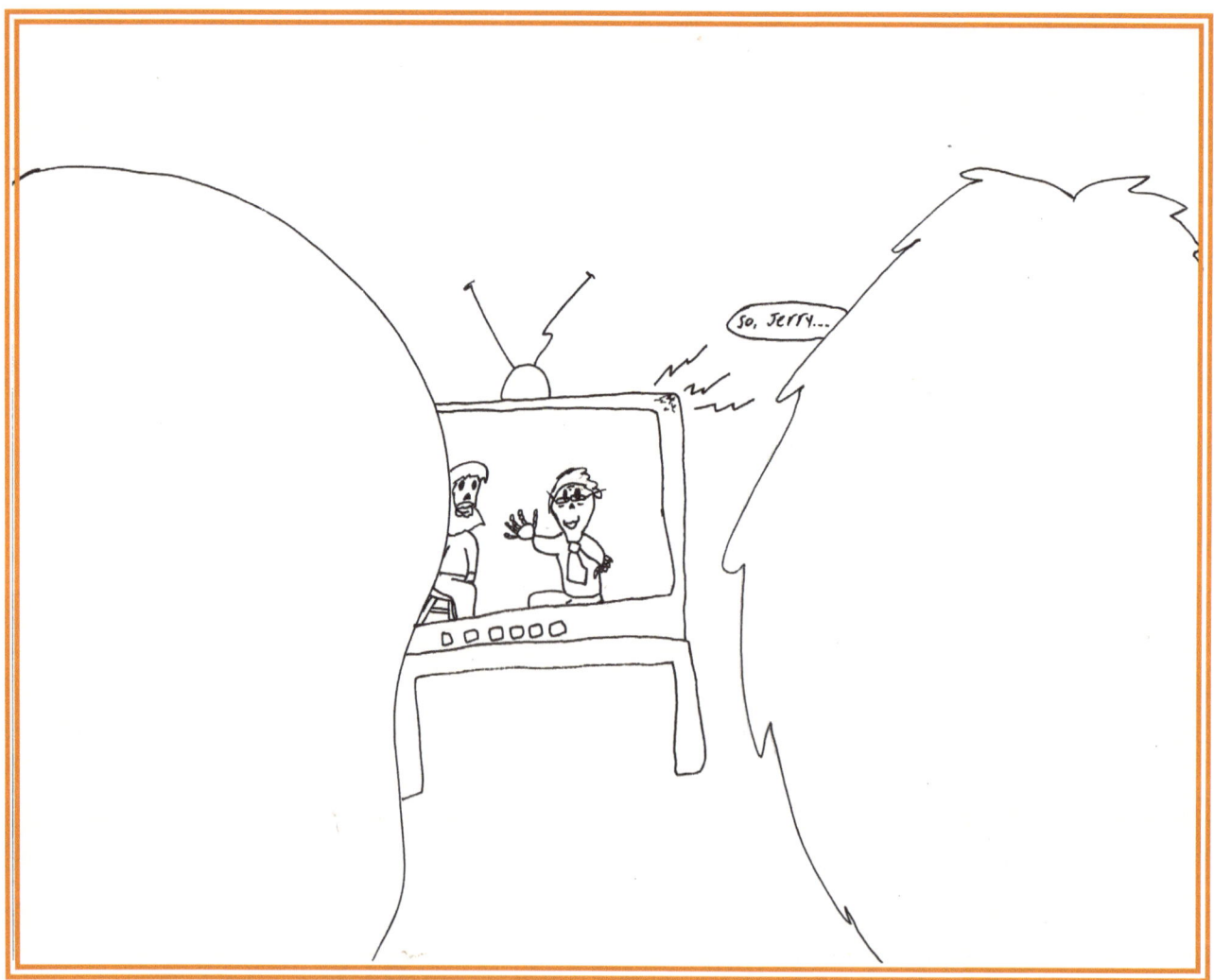

69. The feeling of unity among Deadheads

# 70. Trying to get into a New Year's show.

71. Seeing the older fans still attending shows.

72. The level of creativity at Dead shows.

73. Hearing, "The Music Never Stopped" on a hot day.

74. That feeling of timelessness one has at a Dead show.

75. Knowing that I'd always enjoy the show.

76. The generosity in the hearts of Deadheads.

# 77. Hearing "Sugar Magnolia" live.

78. Hearing about other "Heads" tour stories.

79. Jerry Band shows.

80. Knowing that "The Grateful Dead Experience" is an ongoing entity.

## 81. Surprise shows.

# 82. Building on the number of shows I'd attended.

83. Hearing "Touch Of Grey" live.

84. The encore song(s).

85. Sensing that the show wasn't over until the band actually got into their limos and left the area.

86. Reading the destination points on signs held by departing Dead heads after a show.

# 87. Not getting "smushed" in the front row.

88. Hearing "Throwing Stones" live.

89. Not feeling like rushing off when the show was over.

90. Hearing other Deadheads play songs themselves between shows.

91. Hearing the audience calling out tunes during a show.

# 92. Adding to my Grateful Dead ticket-stub collection.

93. Songs that lead into another such as "China/Rider" live.

94. Seeing various Grateful Dead license plates at shows.

95. Hearing the Dead sing cover-tunes.

## 96. Seeing the Dead play with other musicians.

97. Being at a place where the barter system was so widely accepted.

## 98. Seeing more Grateful Dead music videos.

99. The opportunity to go back stage at a Grateful Dead show.

100.
And finally, I will miss the entire Deadhead Experience known to some of us as, "Grateful Dead Land".

Bob Weir with Author at a fundraiser; Carmel Valley, California - 1991.

www.ingramcontent.com/pod-product-compliance
Lightning Source LLC
Chambersburg PA
CBHW042007150426
43195CB00002B/51